THE COL[...] CATECHISM

by

Vincent J. Cardinal

SAMUEL FRENCH, INC.
45 WEST 25TH STREET   NEW YORK 10010
7623 SUNSET BOULEVARD HOLLYWOOD 90046
LONDON   TORONTO

For

Milan Stitt
&
Ken and Joanne Cardinal

IMPORTANT BILLING AND CREDIT REQUIREMENTS

All producers of *THE COLORADO CATECHISM must* give credit to the Author of the Play in all programs distributed in connection with performances of the Play and in all instances in which the title of the Play appears for purposes of advertising, publicizing or otherwise exploiting the Play and/or a production. The name of the Author *must* also appear on a separate line, on which no other name appears, immediately following the title, and *must* appear in size of type not less than fifty percent the size of the title type.

All producers of *THE COLORADO CATECHISM* must also provide the following billing in any publication, advertisement or production of the play, on the program's title page or on the page thereafter:

"Originally produced by The Circle Repertory Company, New York City, Tanya Berezin, Artistic Director."

The Colorado Catechism was originally produced by The Circle Repertory Company, New York City. Opened October, 1990. Tanya Berezin, Artistic Director. Jody Boese, Production Manager. Mark Ramont, Director. Denise Yaney, Stage Manager. James Youmans, Set Design. David C. Woolard, Costume Design. Pat Dignan, Lighting Design. Steweart Werner & Chuck London, Sound Design.

TY ....Kevin J. O'Connor
DONNA ....Becky Baker

It was subsequently produced by Wandering Bark Productions in association with Margalo Productions, West Hollywood, California. Opened January, 1993. Stephen Burleigh, Producer. Remi Aubuchon, Director. Joe Morrissey, Stage Manager, Lighting & Sound Design. Deborah Raymond & Dorian Vernacchio, Set Design. Durinda Wood, Costume Design.

TY ....Tim Daly
DONNA ....Amy Van Nostrand

CHARACTERS

TY, a financially successful portrait painter in his early thirties.

DONNA, a home economics teacher in her mid-thirties.

SETTING

Ty Wain's painting studio, the present. And the front porch and yard of the Roger Goodman Drug and Alcohol Clinic in the town of Cripple Creek, Colorado. The not-too-distant past.

Reading Note:
The places and the times of the events, *The Studio* and *The Clinic,* are indicated at the beginning of each section as a reading aid. These arbitrary divisions should not be interpreted as scenes. The events of the play follow rapidly upon each other without scene breaks or black outs. The audience does not need to know specific times or dates.

THE COLORADO CATECHISM

ACT I

AT RISE: A large scrim may serve as the canvas for an almost finished painting of a bone-white porch attached to a Victorian House in the Rocky Mountain town of Cripple Creek, Colorado or perhaps the painting is only in progress on the wall in Ty's Studio. Near the porch is a table with the beginnings of a card castle. Although TY refers to a woman on the porch, she is not present. The house is a drug and alcohol treatment center. TY is standing in front of the canvas. The canvas exists in Ty's studio, a rock and roll classic plays on a BOOM BOX which sits on Ty's cluttered paint table. TY, agitated, looks at a playing card—the ace of spades— pockets it. HE turns off the MUSIC, then addresses the audience.

THE STUDIO—July 4th, This Year

TY. A painting. A picture. A portrait. A portrait of a woman. A woman on a porch. A woman on a bone-white Victorian porch. A woman. A portrait of a woman without a woman.

I am a portrait painter. I was a portrait painter. I used to capture the quintessence of a person in a single pose, a moment. I have merchandised, sold and re-sold old images but this portrait of a woman is my first new work in three years. It is to prove to my backers that I am worth the

7

investment again. To prove I can still paint. To prove I can still create. But I can't.

Artie used to say, "Man only has three absolute freedoms, darling. The freedom to love, the freedom to create, and the freedom to die by his own hand. Baby, if you ever lose painting and love, don't be so boring as to ignore suicide."

Why can't I paint her? Why can't I move her from my heart, my head, my hand, to the canvas? Why should I be haunted by her for three years—three years sober and three years haunted? Why? Why?

Questions. Secrets. Games.

June Second. The night before, in Manhattan, my business associates had an "intervention" for me. They told me I was an alcoholic and an addict and that I had hurt them—financially. I was bankrupt. I could still paint then. But I missed deadlines, fought with clients, and, at an opening party, trashed a gallery full of my work. My associates put me on a plane to Cripple Creek, Colorado and The Roger Goodman Clinic for Alcohol And Drug Rehabilitation.

Before the plane landed I lifted a few dozen bottles from the cart. By the time my car got to Cripple Creek most of the bottles were empty. In this "condition," I met Donna. (*TY stands at the clinic—an exact replica of the scene in the painting.*)

THE CLINIC—June 2nd—Three Years Ago

(*DONNA enters from the house, carrying a half eaten Twinkie, walks up to Ty with purpose, and slaps him across the face. SHE realizes she has made a mistake*) *and, without apology, turns and walks back up the stairs.)*

TY. Is this the Treatment Center?

DONNA. A what?

TY. My driver said this was the alcohol rehabilitation center.

DONNA. Go away. Just go away, okay?

TY. Is there somebody inside I could speak to? Is there a receptionist?

DONNA. I'm the receptionist.

TY. Jesus.

DONNA. I'm the receptionist and we are full.

TY. I was told you were expecting me.

DONNA. If I was expecting you would I have slapped you?

TY. I'm, I'm, I'm not sure.

DONNA. I'm not sorry I slapped you and I'm not gonna say I'm sorry, because, I'm just not sorry and to say so would be a lie.

TY. Just, just, just let me talk to the director.

DONNA. He's in with the drunks. He can't be bothered. You look peak-ed.

Want a Twinkie? It's contraband. The Twinkie. This is a nutritionally based center, so there's no sugar except what they give you people at meals. If Roger caught you eating this Twinkie, you'd be in major trouble.

Was that your limousine?

TY. Yes. No, I mean, I took it from the airport. I mean not "took it," but rented it, leased it. Listen, just let me register.

DONNA. I'm on my break.

TY. When is your break over?

DONNA. After I smoke. (*DONNA removes a clip board from beside the door and refers to it for TY's orientation.*) See, the drunks are supposed to be in group right now. Breakfast is at 7:30, Lunch is at 11:30, and Dinner is at 5:30. Television is available from 8:30 to 10:30 and your group meeting will be at 9:30 in the morning and 1:30 in the afternoon. Chores will be assigned to you later. On breaks you have to be in sight of the center room. Don't go taking any walks. Smoking is allowed everywhere, but nothing else you enjoy is. Chimes will ring at the end of each session. Your life is run by chimes. Roger is a Nazi. Do you have a name?

TY. I'm Ty W.

DONNA. Oh, this isn't an A.A. meeting, you can have a last name.

TY. I'd rather people didn't know I'm here.

DONNA. Are you famous?

TY. I'm Ty Wain.

DONNA. I'm Donna Sicard. I'm not famous either.

THE STUDIO

TY. (*To the audience.*) And then then she asked me the C. A. G. E., Cage questions. Questions designed to determine if I was an alcoholic.

THE CLINIC—June 2nd—Afternoon

DONNA. Have you ever felt the need to cut down on your drinking? "Cut" is the word that starts "C" in the CAGE questions.

TY. Yes, I have.

DONNA. Oh, come on.

TY. I have. I think about cutting down a lot.

DONNA. You're just saying that so I'll admit you.

TY. That's enough of your shit, either ask the questions or let me talk to this Roger guy.

DONNA. "Annoyed." Have you ever felt "annoyed" by criticism of your drinking?

TY. Only when it's really unfair.

DONNA. Will you, please be more specific, Mr. Wain?

TY. More specific? Okay ... Like my girlfriend, ex-girlfriend, used to complain about a few drinks with dinner—and that's annoying.

DONNA. Go on.

TY. She poured a pitcher of Margueritas over my head one night at "El Teddy."

DONNA. Why?

TY. She's totally irrational.

DONNA. And ... What did you do?

TY. I threw a bowl of peaches flambé on her.

DONNA. Was it flambé-ing?

TY. It didn't hurt her.

DONNA. You threw fire at your girlfriend in a restaurant?

TY. Jesus, I sound like a real jerk.

DONNA. I think that would count as a "yes."

(A wave of nausea hits TY. HE sits on the front porch stair.)

DONNA. "Eye-opener." Do you ever take a morning "eye-opener"? Are you okay?

TY. Let's just get through this.

DONNA. Morning eye-opener.

TY. I paint at night, all night. I drink when I paint—it helps. Some mornings I have a meeting or something and I've only had two or three hours sleep, so I have something as a continuation of the night's drinking, not a real "eye opener."

I guess the answer's "Yes."

DONNA. I took it as a "yes." Do you have any candy or anything on you?

TY. You forgot "G."

DONNA. "G." "Guilt." How could I forget "guilt"? Catholic Education. Eight years of nuns, four years of priests, twelve years of therapy.

TY. Me too.

DONNA. Oh, I was hoping you wouldn't be Catholic.

TY. I do feel guilty about drinking, sometimes.

DONNA. Of course. Catholic.

TY. Right, I've had guilty feelings about breathing.

DONNA. But that doesn't mean you should quit. Right?

TY. Right. No. I mean. You should keep breathing, not drinking. How come talking to you is so confusing.

DONNA. I have the power to cloud men's minds. It's a necessity with a face like mine. Wanna a cigarette?

TY. No, I quit.

DONNA. There's no sugar here, no sex, and no booze. This is not a good time to squander your vices.

TY. I kept getting ashes in my oil paints.

DONNA. I'm glad it wasn't for your health. You feel any better?

TY. Some.

DONNA. You passed the CAGE test.
TY. Is that it?
DONNA. You're an alcoholic.
TY. Thanks a lot.

THE STUDIO

TY. She was the first person I ever talked to about drinking. But that isn't it. That isn't a portrait. That afternoon, there was a moment. A moment when I think her secrets stopped and our secrets began.

THE CLINIC—June 2nd—Afternoon

DONNA. Hide!

(*DONNA grabs TY and hurries him to the side of the house—out of view of the main window.*)

TY. Why?
DONNA. Prescott's going to take a pee and he'll see you.
TY. So?
DONNA. Quiet! He'll tell Roger you're out here.
TY. Good.
DONNA. You're tanked up.
TY. No I'm not.
DONNA. Then go ahead. Get us both kicked out.
TY. (*Starts for the Clinic's main door.*) I knew you were no receptionist!
DONNA. You're already in big trouble!
TY. Whu ...!?!

DONNA. You're tanked. First impressions with Roger are very important. I can't believe you'd show up at a treatment center drunk. No one has ever done that before. You are a real case.

TY. I'm not drunk.

DONNA. Yes you are.

TY. When, when, when I am drunk, no one can ever tell. This is just altitude sickness.

DONNA. You're just like my Brad. When you are tanked you repeat words three times; "When, when, when I am drunk ..." or "Let me, let me, let me talk to the director ..." or

TY. Okay, okay, okay ...

DONNA. See?

TY. Okay, I drank about three million of those little bottles on the plane. (*Takes out a package of Certs Breath Mints.*)

DONNA. Can I have one of those?

TY. Sure.

DONNA. Thanks. Shoot, they're sugarless. Three million little bottles, your blood alcohol must be through the ceiling.

TY. Are they going to check that?

DONNA. Yes!

TY. Shit.

DONNA. Roger will rip your lips off, but ... everyone gets drunk before they come in.

TY. You lied *again*.

DONNA. I know I lied *again*. I was afraid you'd go in and tell Roger that some loony drunk smacked you up side the head. I couldn't afford that now. Roger doesn't think much of me. See, I'm a run of the mill drunk just like you.

(TY sits on the porch's side steps. DONNA joins him eventually.)

DONNA. You feel any better?

TY. It has just been a long ... Last night was my "intervention." They're all just worried about their money. I just went into Chapter Thirteen.

DONNA. Bankruptcy?

TY. I say Chapter Thirteen to prevent a heart attack.

DONNA. How'd someone as young as you get rich enough to go bankrupt?

TY. I did everything too young, too fast.

DONNA. Everything?

TY. Everything but die.

DONNA. So far.

TY. So far.

DONNA. If you're bankrupt ...

TY. Do you have to keep saying that?

DONNA. If you are, how come you came here in a limousine?

TY. They let you budget the lifestyle you're accustomed to before the creditors dig in.

DONNA. Shoot, I could get accustomed to limousines.

TY. Money doesn't make you happy.

DONNA. No, but it makes suffering pretty comfortable.

TY. *(Crosses away from Donna.)* Look, last night I almost killed myself. While I was cleaning up the studio, putting the paint away, protecting the finished ones, I thought, I thought about, I thought about just eating all my colors, all my paint. Sucking down tube after tube of burnt sienna, and umber, and trinity, and emerald green. Just taking it all in and when they cut me open to see how I died they'd see the most beautiful gut of colors just spilling all out, all over me.

DONNA. Death isn't that complicated when you really want it. Death is easy, unless you have a six year old. You started drinking last night, didn't you. Didn't you? Did it taste better thinking it was your last binge forever?

TY. I drank all the dribs and drabs of whiskey and vodka and liqueurs—wild boozy colors. Artie used to call it "going for God." Getting so high, God would be in reach.

DONNA. (*Comforts Ty by rubbing his arm.*) I can still smell God on your breath.

TY. I'm sure.

DONNA. If you stay, even one night, you're going to need God.

TY. Is it going to be that bad?

DONNA. Withdrawal? Yes! If you don't die—you'll die a little—a person can die a little.

(*DONNA holds Ty for a moment. HE then kisses her. DONNA's kiss becomes deeper and almost violent. TY begins to struggle, pulling away.*)

TY. You're trying to taste it!
DONNA. No!
TY. You're like those women who drink vanilla extract!
DONNA. I'm telling Roger! (*DONNA exits into the clinic, leaving TY to address the audience.*)

THE STUDIO

TY. She didn't tell Roger. The actual receptionist was far less friendly than Donna. After a battery of questions— none of which I could answer to her satisfaction—she told me to empty my pockets. She took my checkbook, credit cards, cash and Certs. She said, "How am I supposed to know they aren't L.S.D.?" I kept some secret cash stashed in my shoe—for emergencies. Withdrawal started late that night—it was the week long hangover I'd been avoiding for fifteen years. She was there every moment. Caring and talking ... and talking.

(DONNA sits on the front step. TY, trembling moves onto all fours as if he has the dry heaves.)

THE CLINIC, Early June 3rd

DONNA. I wanted to go to the prom.

TY. I would listen and shake ...

DONNA. The day before the prom, I got a note in my locker that said, ...

TY. ... and she'd talk ...

DONNA. "Dearest Donna, Will you go to the prom with me?"

TY. ... and I'd vomit ... and she'd talk. She was *always* there.

(TY sits back as DONNA comforts him and talks.)

DONNA. "Love, Jean-Marc."

He was the most beautiful boy in the world. I got that note and I cut my afternoon classes and I went home and I got a tall glass of milk, and a bag of Oreos, and got in my bed and watched the Prize Movie on Channel Forty-three, all afternoon. I was beautiful with Oreos in my bed and Jean-Marc in my head.

My mama helped me make my own dress, a strapless top that fit real tight and then swooshed out at the bottom, and Mama spent twenty dollars on my hair-do and nails. I said I was sure Jean-Marc was the kind of boy who would buy a wrist corsage for his prom date, so Mama gave me her silver bracelet—that Daddy had given her—for my other wrist. That night I posed for pictures all dressed up in my prom clothes and I waited by the window, and I waited at the end of the driveway and I waited at the top of the street.

But it was a joke all along. I knew that note wasn't real. The hand writing was just too girlie. But I couldn't go back home, because I knew Mama would be disappointed in me. So, I walked to the baseball diamond and sat down in the bleachers until I could go home and pretend I had been to the prom.

I told my Brad, my husband, that I'd fall in love with the man who gave me a wrist corsage and you know what he did? He said, "I'll kill the S.O.B. that gives my woman a corsage." Want some soup? (*DONNA exits to make soup.*)

TY. (*To audience.*) Finally, by the third day. I could talk back.

<u>THE CLINIC—June 5th, 2:10 a.m.</u>

(*DONNA appears at the door.*)

TY. Go away.

(DONNA exits. CHIMES ring. Here, and throughout the play, THEY acknowledge the sound of the chimes— always a rude interruption. TY talks from downstage left.)

TY. Chimes. I remember the chimes. Ringing each hour all day until midnight—then silence. Then it was safe to roam around—unless Roger was prowling. Roger was unpredictable and always awake.

(CHIMES. DONNA joins TY, also standing.)

THE CLINIC—June 6th, 12:00 a.m.

TY. I wish you'd quit following me everywhere I go.
DONNA. I don't follow you everywhere you go.
TY. You followed me to the bathroom.
DONNA. I always come out here at night.
TY. I was here first.
DONNA. Roger will give you bloody hell if he finds you out here with a woman in the middle of the night. He tossed Mark and Jeni out like yesterday's newspaper. Mark said he was just looking for something in Jeni's eye. Roger said he *heard* them kissing. He *heard* them. He must have a sonar for sex sounds. When Mark left, he went down to the Red Rooster Bar and bought rounds for everybody. They said he signed Roger's name to the tab. Roger *heard* Jeni and Mark kissing. Can you believe that?
TY. Go back to bed before he hears you.

DONNA. I'm not kissing. There's Chamomile tea in the kitchen. That's relaxing.

TY. I'm fine.

DONNA. I'll make it for you.

TY. You know, you're the kind of person that would give a man directions to his own house.

DONNA. Only if he needed them. (*DONNA exits. CHIMES ring.*)

<u>THE CLINIC—June 7th, 2:10 a.m.</u>

(*TY sits down right on a tree stump. DONNA enters from the house, but doesn't see him at first.*)

DONNA. You should put on a coat, you're gonna catch a pneumonia out here.

TY. I'm fine.

DONNA. It's practically snowing.

TY. I'm fine, okay?

DONNA. (*Puts an afghan around his shoulders then crosses to her card castle.*) I bet the moonlight'll make snow diamonds. Shoot, snow in June. Sweet Mary, the wind has knocked over my cards. This part's wrecked.

You still vomiting like you were?

You were having another nightmare.

TY. So?

DONNA. What about?

TY. Nothing.

DONNA. What is your nightmare about?

TY. I don't remember dreams.

DONNA. Just so you know, Roger would call this "emotional stuffing."

TY. I don't remember dreams.

DONNA. Do to. You're being evasive. You never say anything real. You say things like you're here because your business associates want you to be here. That's evasive. That's no reason to dry out. You're too old to be here for the "grown-ups."

TY. Grown-ups? Who do you think makes it possible to have the limousine that you find so fucking impressive? The "grown-ups" account. They promote. They represent. The "grown-ups" are my life. Don't give me shit about why I'm here—I'm here to save my life.

DONNA. I'd say with the kind of symptoms you have, you probably did cocaine. Didn't you? Didn't you do cocaine?

TY. Mind your own business.

DONNA. You did.

TY. Get lost.

DONNA. Did.

TY. Didn't.

DONNA. Did too.

TY. Forget it.

DONNA. Did. (*Exits.*)

THE STUDIO

TY. She was worse than a twelve year old!

THE CLINIC—June 6th, 2:10 a.m.

DONNA. (*From offstage.*) Did.

(CHIMES. TY looks to the door expecting Donna. SHE doesn't enter. HE waits. Finally DONNA enters.)

THE CLINIC—June 8th, 2:10 a.m.

TY. You know, you don't have to meet me here every night.

DONNA. I know.

TY. You're later than usual. (*Leans against the porch post by the front stairs.*)

DONNA. I was writing my son Devan a letter.

He's at summer camp. I'd never drink Devan's vanilla extract, you were wrong about that. I'm a good mother. (*Sits in the stage left chair.*) By the time I decided to come here, I was just drinking white wine. A lot of white wine. For awhile I only took Valium. It's sort of like dried Vodka in pill form. You know that old joke? Alcoholism is a Valium deficiency?

TY. I don't get it.

DONNA. Rehab humor. This is my third time.

TY. Three times?

DONNA. After the first time, my first time in rehab, I got home and looked around, everything was, I don't know, different—like it was someone else's couch and kitchen and husband. This man in my bed was a bloated boy who still ate Lucky Charms and Pepsi Cola for breakfast.

See, I fell in love with the high school baseball star. Unfortunately, I was a high school teacher by then.

He fell for me. I don't know why.

After rehab, I just didn't know where I was, or who I was, or why I was.

So, I had a few drinks and I really felt better. I thought, damn it, this is why I drink, because when I drink I know where I am, and who I am, and why I am.

TY. I did a hell of a lot more than white wine.

DONNA. Oh, I know. You're a "hard drinker" or you "really hold your liquor" or whatever those macho things are that you say, but the hand that rocks the cradle isn't supposed to tip the bottle—unless it's to fill her man's glass.

TY. If you've been in rehabilitation three times, you might have a real problem.

DONNA. Don't worry, it's not contagious. If you've got one—it's all your own.

TY. Good. Now you understand. You keep your problems to yourself and I'll keep mine to myself.

DONNA. Don't go telling me anymore of your business either. I don't want to know it. (*Exits into the house.*)

THE STUDIO

TY. She wanted to know *all* my business. In the beginning most of us held on to our problems like they were all we owned. My roommate, Dooley, didn't even talk to me until the seventh day—then at two a. m., as I snuck out to see Donna again, he spoke—well actually, hiding under his sheet—he sang:

Goin' up Cripple Creek, Goin' at a whirl
Goin' up Cripple Creek to see my girl

(*TY crosses tree stump and sits.*) I think that's the first time I thought of her as "My girl." I totally denied it to Dooley. I told him to "fuck off." As I left he was singing:

(*DONNA enters from the fence down right. TY doesn't see her.*)

TY. (*Singing.*)
Got me a gal, 'bout half grown
Jumps on a man like a dog on a bone

THE CLINIC—June 9th, 2:10 a.m.

DONNA. What are you singing?
TY. One of Dooley's dumb songs.
DONNA. So he's finally talking?
TY. Just singing.
DONNA. Sweet Mary.
TY. It's really dark up here.
DONNA. Stars are brighter.
TY. Because it's so dark, they seem brighter.
DONNA. It's because we're closer to them.
TY. No. Two miles in the whole universe is nothing.
DONNA. I believe it's something, just look at how much brighter the stars are.
TY. (*Frustrated.*) It's just dark.
DONNA. My mama used to say that a shooting star signals the beginning of something grand.
TY. Did you see one?
DONNA. No. Shh!
TY. Why?
DONNA. I thought I heard someone.

TY. Just the wind.

DONNA. It's chilly.

TY. That's the mountains.

DONNA. I feel like we're fifteen year olds coming home late from a first date.

TY. I didn't really date at fifteen.

DONNA. (*In frustration.*) Me neither, but can't you just imagine?

TY. Not really.

Before you came out here, that's what fifteen was like for me.

DONNA. Did your parents drink?

TY. No. Sort of.

DONNA. Sort of?

TY. My dad went out every night and had fun while my mom stayed home and worried about his drinking.

DONNA. Who are you most like?

TY. Who would you pick?

DONNA. I hope my son doesn't pick Brad or me. I want my son to be like ... Hell, it's scary when you can't even think who you want your kid to be like ...

TY. It's scary. It's all scary out there ... The only good thing about being in this place is you don't have to be out there. Jesus.

DONNA. "Jesus has nothing to do with it." That's what Sister Rose would say. She believed in this sort of wild God that wasn't bad or vengeful, just untamed. You know, like the wind, while he was fixing up some great miracle in this corner of the universe, he forgot that he left that storm brewing or those people dying or those men killing. A sort of undependable, enthusiastic God.

TY. I'm not good at the God stuff. I don't obey well.

DONNA. But you're a painter, a creator—like God—
"creator" of the universe. Not "obeyer" of the universe.

TY. I'm glad you came out here. I am.

(A LIGHT goes on inside the house.)

DONNA. Oh, sweet Mary, Roger's on the prowl.
Don't even lick your lips! He hears lips.
Ty, you go in and say you were having a smoke.

TY. But I don't smoke.

DONNA. Start now.

TY. We aren't doing anything ...

(DONNA tosses TY her cigarettes—Camel unfiltered.)

DONNA. You've got nothing to lose. This is the end
of the line for me.

TY. Maybe he's just after a cup of tea.

DONNA. It's us he's after. Light up. I'll go around the
back.

TY. But ...

DONNA. Don't tell. *(Escapes behind the house.)*

THE STUDIO

TY. *(To Donna.)* Wait! *(To the audience.)* We were
breaking rules and it was electrifying. I had missed this
simple thrill, the innocent evil in being with a girl, on a
porch, too late at night.

(CHIMES. Time changes. DONNA enters, with a coffee cup, and sits in a chair and begins working on the card castle.)

<u>THE CLINIC—June 9th, 8:30 a.m.</u>

DONNA. It's not a castle, just a house, a cottage even. Maybe a hut.

TY. *(Joins Donna, but remains standing.)* I could help you build the house, cottage.

DONNA. Hut.

TY. Hut?

DONNA. Hut.

TY. Can I?

DONNA. No. You're still shaking too much.

TY. I'm not shaking.

DONNA. You don't understand. One little mess up makes it all fall down.

TY. What's your name?

DONNA. You don't remember my name?

TY. I'm not good at names.

DONNA. You remembered long enough to tell Roger who you were talking to.

TY. No, I didn't.

DONNA. He's been looking at me in that side-long way, like you told him.

TY. I didn't even see him.

DONNA. I don't think we have a chance for a very positive relationship. So, maybe you should just forget we ever met.

TY. I'm not asking you to sleep with me.

DONNA. There is a rule about not having relationships.

TY. Sexual relationships. I just want to know your name.

DONNA. You flirt with everyone, with everything. You've flirted your way through your whole life because you got that face and those eyes.

TY. I have not flirted with you. I have not even been nice to you.

DONNA. Okay, you can help, but if you mess it up that's all you get to do. One mess up and you go in and watch TV.

(TY sits in the other chair and joins DONNA in building the card castle. The first card TY tenderly tries to put on the card castle is the ace of spades.)

DONNA. No. Holy Mary, give me patience.

TY. What?

DONNA. Don't put the ace of spades on yet. That goes on the top when the castle's finished.

TY. Ah, ha! Castle! You said, "castle."

DONNA. Okay, maybe I aspire to a castle. But the ace of spades would go on top of a hut also.

TY. You've got six decks of cards there. Just use an ace from one of those.

DONNA. No. It has to be from the foundation deck.

(THEY work in silence for a moment.)

TY. Estelle is a nice person.

DONNA. You're good at her name.

TY. She really lights up when she sees me.

DONNA. She lights up when she sees me too.

TY. Oh.

DONNA. She's very friendly to everyone.

TY. That's a good quality.

DONNA. She's a stewardess.

TY. There's nothing wrong with being a stewardess.

DONNA. No. And there's nothing wrong with being perky.

TY. Stewardesses go through a lot of training.

DONNA. She probably downed her share of those little bottles of whiskey.

TY. Don't remind me.

DONNA. If I were her I'd have hidden some of those little bottles in the lining of my luggage.

TY. Like the Twinkies?

DONNA. *(Ironically.)* Sweet Mary, it's a joy to be sober.

TY. It will keep you from dying.

DONNA. No, everyone dies. It'll keep you from falling apart. Not everyone falls apart.

TY. That's the worst part. I did, I already did fall apart or I wouldn't be here.

DONNA. You told him didn't you?

TY. No, I didn't say anything to him.

DONNA. Did you fall apart because of alcohol and cocaine?

TY. Is your father Sam Donaldson or what? Yes, both. Yes. I did cocaine.

DONNA. I knew you did.

If you ever drink, I don't want to know you. Okay?

TY. Okay.

DONNA. It would kill me to see you drunk again. It scared me.

TY. Okay.

DONNA. Okay.

TY. I did see Roger. But I didn't say anything.

DONNA. I saw you see him. I was in the kitchen. I think you, now maybe unconsciously, but you did sort of pull a face like this ... in my direction.

TY. I didn't even know you were in the kitchen.

DONNA. Where did you think I would go if I ran around to the back door which leads into the kitchen?

TY. I wasn't thinking, okay? I'm a very sick person, right now.

DONNA. Inside they'd accuse you of "playing for sympathy."

TY. Like your prom story? Wasn't that "playing for sympathy?"

DONNA. It was. It was for sympathy and it wasn't true. It wasn't.

TY. What?

DONNA. All the feelings were true, just not the incidents.

TY. Jesus, you just sort of lie randomly.

DONNA. When I tell the truth, there's not much to say.

TY. Does that mean you were lying when you said we don't have a chance for a positive rela ... (*TY, too shaky, knocks over part of the card castle.*)

DONNA. What did I say? What did I say would happen?

TY. I didn't do that.

DONNA. You did. You and your shaky drunk hands. You're trying to do too much, too soon. You should just sit there and recover like everyone else does and not force yourself on other people.

TY. Oh, so now I force myself on people? You, you vampire, practically bit my tongue out of my mouth.

DONNA. So, you've managed to remember that? You manage to recall everything that's flattering and lovely.

TY. If it leaves scars, it's difficult to forget.

DONNA. Well, at least I remembered *you*.

TY. Christ, I remember you, just not your name.

DONNA. I don't think you tried very hard.

TY. Mona, Rhonda ...

DONNA. Rhonda is such a fat name.

TY. Rhoda?

DONNA. Fatter.

TY. Nona, Dinah, Diana,

DONNA. Hotter. On-a, On-a ...

TY. Dionna.

DONNA. Sizzling.

TY. Aunia!?!

DONNA. Freezing.

TY. Shit. Help! Help me. No. Don't help me. Just tell me. I'm no good at this game. I'm paying attention. I'm on the edge of my seat.

DONNA. Go back to bed.

TY. I can't sleep anymore.

DONNA. Roger will see you out here and assign you to chores tomorrow.

TY. (*Crosses to the front door. Yelling.*) Roger's a Nazi!

DONNA. Ty! Shh, he'll hear you.

TY. (*Yelling.*) Rhoda said, "Roger's a Nazi!"

DONNA. I don't think you're funny. I wish you'd leave me alone. Go to bed.

TY. Really?

DONNA. Really.

TY. (*Starts to exit into the house but stops at the door.*) It's just ... I keep having this nightmare ...

DONNA. You said, you don't remember dreams.

TY. It's about, about those last days in New York with Artie.

DONNA. You said you were with the Peach Flambé Lady.

TY. Julie. Artie's ancient history. I was just a kid when we met. Sixteen, sixteen years old. And all alone in the big scary city. Scary and sexy. I used to go to the clubs and get tanked up, you said that. You said "tanked up."

I'd just blast out onto the dance floor. A heroic, nuclear, adolescent melt-down. And they'd all watch—the pretty, the ugly, the lonely, the loved—they'd watch me burn.

Somebody'd buy me a drink. Somebody'd offer me a joint. Somebody'd take me home. It was a way to get by, ya know. Men, women, black, white, old, young—I'd go with anybody.

One grey afternoon I woke up at Artie's. He was just a little older than I am now. I figured I'd eat and leave, maybe get a few bucks, just like every other day, but Artie gave me my own bed, bought me paint, even made the back of the loft a studio for me. Artie showed me colors. Colors and light, texture, space, line, vision. Artie gave me vision.

Artie taught me to paint, to be an artist. He kept me in liquor, coke, pills, anything I wanted. He got galleries to show my stuff and became my manager. He made me rich. Artie made me.

I used to always dream about the fire. He caused it, smoking and drinking. I couldn't get him out through the smoke and heat so I left him there, out cold from liquor and pills. I ran out into the street, half dressed, barefoot. I left black soot tracks in the white snow. I could see where I had been—Artie burned.

DONNA. Sweet Mary.

TY. Here, in the nightmare here, I dream about the horrible, heavy, sound of his breath late at night— before the fire, after he "got sick." I'm sure he's dying there, sweating and dying there in the pitch-black and I don't know what to do for him. I lie next to him—staring at the ceiling, hearing him die and I shiver and shiver and pray to God to make him wake up and be alive. And then ... it isn't Artie breathing, it's me. See, in the nightmare, I am sweating all the life out of me—alone in a cold bed. Anyone who ever loved me, I mean really loved me is dead.

DONNA. Donna. My name is Donna Sicard.

TY. Donna? I said, "Donna" and you said, "No."

DONNA. No you didn't.

TY. I did!

DONNA. You never said, "Donna."

TY. I don't want to play with you, anyway, you cheat.

DONNA. I never cheat.

TY. You lie.

DONNA. Yes, I lie, but I don't cheat.

TY. How am I supposed to know you're not lying about that?

DONNA. I guess you never know, Ty. Not really. Anyway, you were a backslide for me. I rarely lie anymore.

Only when I'm finishing detox and intimidated by rich, handsome, drunks who arrive in limousines.

TY. You think I'm ...

DONNA. Intimidating. I thought you were intimidating. After you've seen someone go through what you did for this week—shaking in bed, hugging the toilet, losing your guts—you can't really think they're too intimidating or ...

TY. Handsome?

DONNA. What? Are you running for homecoming king? Are you campaigning for my affections?

TY. Your report card said, "Does not play well with others" didn't it? Well, if you don't want to play with me you can just go inside and watch TV with the rest of the children.

DONNA. Excuse me? I'm sorry? Did you say I could go inside? You may leave.

TY. No.

DONNA. I'll complain to Roger that you are harassing me.

TY. Go ahead.

DONNA. Okay, I will.

TY. Roger!

DONNA. What are you doing?

TY. Calling Roger. Roger!

DONNA. I'm calling Roger.

(TY leaps up and moves to the front door. DONNA tries to physically stop him.)

TY. I'm calling Roger first.

DONNA. Why? Why are you calling Roger when I'm calling Roger to tell on you?

TY. Because I'm calling Roger to tell on you! Roger!

DONNA. Telling what?

TY. Roger!!

DONNA. What are you telling?

TY. Twinkie. Contraband.

DONNA. Twinkie?

TY. Roger!

DONNA. No. No! I told you about the Twinkie in strictest confidence.

TY. Roger!

DONNA. You are so adolescent.

TY. I know!

DONNA. That wasn't a compliment.

TY. Can I stay here? Roger!

DONNA. Yes, okay, stay, sit, talk.

(THEY return to the chairs.)

TY. Donna. Donna, you have a son, Bob and a husband, Darren.

DONNA. Son, Devan. Husband, Brad. I threw out the rest of the Hostess Products. I did.

TY. It's okay, Roger left about fifteen minutes ago.

DONNA. No!

TY. Yes!

DONNA. *(Punches Ty.)* You ....! I thought you were going to tell on me.

TY. Donna, you can trust me, Scout's Honor.

DONNA. Would you trust you if you were me?

TY. Absolutely.

DONNA. Me too. I'd trust you if I were me. And I am me. I just never thought I could trust an alcoholic again.

TY. Is Brad a drunk too?

DONNA. Ty, don't even try to bring Brad into our relationship.

TY. How can we be friends if you won't talk about Brad?

DONNA. Just not now, okay.

TY. Is there something wrong between you two?

DONNA. Everything is fine.

TY. What's he like?

DONNA. Youthful.

TY. Can I meet him on family day?

DONNA. I don't want to talk about him. Okay?

TY. Isn't this "emotional stuffing"?

DONNA. No. It is a clear sense of personal boundaries.

TY. Ooooookay.

DONNA. Are you ambisexual?

TY. What?

DONNA. Are you ambisexual?

TY. What's that?

DONNA. What's that? You're asking me? I'm from Indiana.

TY. Ambisexual—You mean, do I do it with both hands?

DONNA. Both sexes.

TY. Bisexual.

DONNA. Are you?

TY. Does it matter?

Does it matter?

(CHIMES ring. DONNA walks away into the house. TY calls after her.)

TY. Donna, does it matter?
Does it matter!?!

(TY, agitated, addresses the audience.)

THE STUDIO

TY. The chimes rang and she walked away like Pavlov's fucking dog! Artie Was Right. I am a painter who can not paint—I am nothing. I can't paint her.

(DONNA speaks as if in group. SHE is seen through the window of the house.)

THE CLINIC, June 9th, 8:30 p.m.

DONNA. *(Angry.)* At sixteen, he was tragic and beautiful ...

THE STUDIO

TY. *(Still in his studio.)* No! I am done remembering.
DONNA. And I was plain and angry ...
TY. You only talked about Brad in group. What's the use of remembering him?
DONNA. I was plain and angry and wanted only to take care of him ... all of those boys. Because, damn it, if I

can't satisfy you, I can care for you more than any pretty girl can.

[NOTE: The following sequence should flow smoothly without blackouts. The actors should move into their next positions during the scene rather than between the scenes. A change in the quality of lighting will indicate time passing.]

TY. She had locked me out. For the next few days, I was knocking to get in. We had chores together. Officially, "chores" were called "therapeutic duties"—exercises in being in the right place at the right time.

(DONNA beats a rug stage downstage right.)

<u>THE CLINIC—June 10th, 10:30 a.m.</u>

DONNA. You're late.

TY. (*Picks up broom as he speaks, and starts sweeping the porch.*) I didn't know I'd be working with you. Don't tell Roger. Okay? Did you see the shirt Dooley was wearing in the meeting?

DONNA. No.

TY. It was really funny.

DONNA. I didn't see it.

TY. I'm glad he's my roommate.

DONNA. I liked what you said about drugs quieting secrets. I did.

TY. Thanks.

(A CHIME rings. Time passes. DONNA digs angrily in a flower pot, sitting on the stage right stairs. TY watches from the bench behind her.)

THE CLINIC—June 12th, 2:30 p.m.

TY. Roger was kind of hard on you in the meeting.

DONNA. He doesn't like me because I won't fall for his dog and pony show. It's like the old woman's shoe here, "had so many children, she didn't know what to do..."

TY. You sat with him at lunch.

DONNA. He sat with me.

TY. Did you give him a piece of your mind?

DONNA. He ate my potato chips.

(A CHIME rings. Time passes. TY paints the roof of the porch while DONNA scrapes the down stage right post.)

THE CLINIC—June 13th, 10:30 a.m.

TY. I don't enjoy painting anymore. I'm not a painter. It's just something I do well. I also clean very well, but I'm not a maid. It's like saying, I'm a secretary because Roger has me alphabetizing files.

DONNA. You conned your way into the personal files?

(DONNA exits behind the house in a huff. TY doesn't notice.)

TY. The real thing is I have to drink to paint. I'm only good when I'm tanked. It's not what I am. They just call me a painter ...

(A CHIME rings. Time passes. DONNA enters from inside the house with a several trash bags. TY helps her deposit them behind the fence.)

THE CLINIC—June 14th, 8:30 p.m.

DONNA. I slapped you because, I actually thought you were Brad coming to visit me.
TY. I look like Brad?
DONNA. Not at all.
TY. Why did you think ...
DONNA. I wasn't wearing my contacts.
TY. I'm not wearing any underwear.
DONNA. I am.

(A CHIME rings. Time passes. DONNA snaps beans on the stump. TY peels potatoes on the bench.)

THE CLINIC—June 15th, 2:30 p.m.

DONNA. *(Snacking on the beans.)* I'm one of the teachers with candy on her desk. Not for the kids, for me. Sometimes, when I'm ridiculously selfish, I put the bowl in my drawer so they won't eat it all. I'm a perpetual eater. Snack. Snack. Snack.
TY. What kind of candy?
DONNA. M&Ms.
TY. Plain or peanut?

DONNA. No.

TY. Plain or peanut?

DONNA. No, no, no. I'm not gonna become your candy substitute. No way. You suffer alone on this one.

TY. I'm not craving sweets.

DONNA. I know that desperation.

TY. I was just being polite. Artie used to tell me to engage the buyers in conversations about what they're interested in—try to make conversation. I was trying to make ...

DONNA. Well, make conversation about something other than M&Ms.

TY. Do you remember rootbeer floats?

DONNA. Now who's talking desperate? Hey, listen, first you crave sweets and then you get a blinding need for booze. This morning I could have swallowed Listerine with a cologne chaser if I had it.

Peanut. Not plain. Peanut—for their nutritional value.

(The CHIMES ring. Time passes. TY follows DONNA in with a laundry basket full of sheets. THEY fold sheets in the downstage left area.)

THE CLINIC—June 16th, 6:30 p.m.

TY. I wrote it down, the "Reflection For the Day" you read.

DONNA. Because I read it?

TY. Because I liked it.

DONNA. Do you remember it?

TY. Yes.

DONNA. Well?

TY. Well, what?

DONNA. Say it.

TY. Okay, It said, you said, "It takes courage to grow up and share who we really are."

DONNA. Wrong. You are so wrong. "It takes courage to grow up and *become* who we really are."

TY. You said, "share who we really are."

DONNA. "Sharing" has nothing to do with it. Your ego is so enormous you actually believe my health depends on sharing with you.

TY. I do not have an enormous ego.

DONNA. Oh, my gosh. You are bent over with the weight of your ego. Don't think I haven't seen you, for hours in front of the mirror trying to look thrown together, trying to look artistically unkempt. You are the most pretentious, ego centered person I've ever met.

TY. Me? Me? I get off a plane after having my entire life fall apart and you tell me stories about senior prom and eighteen-year-old lovers. You expect me to memorize your name. You burden me with your entire life—and on top of that it's ALL a lie!

DONNA. Brad is not a lie.

TY. Brad is not a lie? Where is your wedding ring? Why does your file say single? no children?

DONNA. Those files are private ...

TY. How come Brad didn't bring you here? Where was Brad on your Family Day? I know women like you. Phantom husbands and children to protect you from, not men, no, not me, to protect you from life.

DONNA. Brad's dead.

TY. Brad's dead.

Then why did you think I was him?

DONNA. Ghosts.

TY. Jesus. You talk about him like he's alive.

DONNA. Well, it feels like ... it feels like he's dead.

TY. And he is? Brad is dead?

DONNA. No.

TY. How could you lie about that? You're really fucked in the head.

DONNA. It would be easier if he were dead.

TY. Do you feel that way about Devan too? Do you wish Devan was dead too?

DONNA. They took Devan away from me!!

TY. Donna, I'm sorry.

DONNA. That's the way it is. Out there the people you love disappear. Now you know. I thought because I prayed and went to church and really helped kids, you know, made their lives better, that this would not happen to me. That God—even a wild careless god—would not punish me for being good. But then look what he let happen to His own Son.

I came here for my son, Devan.

TY. Roger wants you to do it for yourself.

DONNA. They've already got you, don't they?

TY. I'm just giving A.A. a chance.

DONNA. Well, Brad gave it a fucking chance and they didn't help him.

TY. From what Roger says ...

DONNA. Wake up. This is all Roger's addiction. This place, these meetings, us. Roger just traded one addiction for another. Roger is still addicted.

TY. But not to alcohol, not to drugs, not to the things that destroyed you and Brad.

DONNA. A.A. wasn't there when Brad hit my little boy.

TY. Well, Where were you!?!

DONNA. Does it matter?!? Does it matter?!?

TY. Yes! Yes, to me it matters! To me, you matter!

DONNA. They sent me the papers today. I have to go to custody court in Indiana.

TY. Why did they take him away from you?

DONNA. July fifth, the trial is July fifth.

TY. Donna, did you do something to Devan?

DONNA. Holy Mary, I could use a drink right now.

TY. Donna?

DONNA. They take kids away from alcoholics in Indiana.

TY. Jesus. There is no summer camp in Maine then?

DONNA. No. No summer camp. No.

TY. No summer camp. Jesus.

DONNA. Shit.

TY. Will Brad be at the trial?

DONNA. Brad left us—me.
I never said that sober before today, "Brad left me." Brad's dead to me.

TY. But you're not dead.

DONNA. Do you have any of the little bottles from the plane?

TY. No. I don't have any little bottles.

DONNA. It's all so unfair. They way things turn out. Did you just say, "You're not dead"?

TY. Yes.

DONNA. I hate it when drunks start talking like Hallmark cards.

TY. You've seen a Hallmark card that says, "You're not dead"?

(CHIMES. DONNA exits. TY addresses the audience from his studio.)

THE STUDIO

TY. There was no grasping her truth ...
Until that night, when I found a note around my tooth brush.

(DONNA is isolated by LIGHT near the door to the house.)

THE CLINIC—June 16th, 10:30 p.m.

DONNA. Dear Ty,
Here is the truth:
One. Brad lives with a waitress in Cincinnati.
Two. Devan is in foster care in Indiana and I'm scared I'm going to lose him forever. I'm scared.
Three. You do matter to me. You do matter.
Your friend,
Donna
TY. P.S.
DONNA. "It does take courage to grow up and *share* ...

THE STUDIO

TY. ... and share who we really are." If I loved her, I mean really loved her, I would have gone to her then. I would have held her, kissed her, told her not to be scared.

That I loved her. I didn't. I could never really love. "Baby, if you ever lose painting *and* love, don't be so boring as to ignore ..."

She said, "Death isn't that complicated, when you really want it." (*TY tastes the paint as the LIGHTS fade to BLACK.*)

End of ACT I

[*NOTE:* The Colorado Catechism *may be played without an intermission by deleting "She said, 'Death isn't that complicated, when you really want it.' " from the last part of Act I and the first part of Act II.*]

ACT II

(TY is in the studio where we left him at the end of Act I.)

THE STUDIO

TY. "Death isn't that complicated, when you really want it." But the kind of death Artie would have wanted, the "well crafted death" is an art. I will eat all my colors. I will stand in front of this empty portrait and Bang! Bang! Bang!—splatter my guts all out, all over the canvas. The ultimate painting—the "Suicide's Self Portrait."

THE CLINIC—June 17th, 2:30 p.m.

DONNA. Ty, please, draw me svelte.

TY. I never drew you.

DONNA. With voluptuous lips.

TY. I never drew you!

DONNA. Not realistic like the last one you did.

TY. If I could draw you I wouldn't be considering ...

DONNA. Devan draws me all the time.

TY. I thought if I stayed sober I'd be rewarded. Sobriety would take away all my problems. At least I could paint when I was drunk.

DONNA. Devan draws me with a fat round body—long stick legs and a big pancake face without any mouth. That's his father's influence.

TY. I did ... I did draw when I was sober—at the clinic. I got her truthful note and I started drawing again. I drew

47

like I was seeing for the first time; rocks, trees, clouds, shoes and I drew Donna. Why can't I now?

(Time passes. TY and DONNA recline on a picnic blanket stage left of the house. As the time shifts, so do their positions. Through out, TY sketches DONNA on a place mat.)

THE CLINIC—June 17th

DONNA. Erica was the Anal Retentive poster child. Holy Mother Mary! She wouldn't break a rule if her life depended on it. One time Father Randal was passing back our chemistry note books. Somehow he held hers over a Bunsen burner. Erica's hand shot up in the air. She waved her hand, bouncing up and down in her seat. The notebook smoldered. Father Randal wouldn't call on her so she wouldn't talk. The note book burned. She's a brain surgeon now.

(Time passes.)

THE CLINIC—June 18th

TY. I was a good son. I didn't visit much.
DONNA. Much?
TY. I visited when my mom was sick. My father said, "What's your life like now?" and I glanced out the window and he said, "It's okay, you've got other people to see."

(Time passes.)

THE CLINIC—June 19th

DONNA. My mama took me into the closet and said, "Don't tell anyone, but I'm really Sleeping Beauty."

(Time passes.)

THE CLINIC—June 20th

TY. If I put a hat on the bed, or killed a spider, or spilled the salt—Artie would go through the roof. He was so superstitious that he wouldn't ever say "Goodbye" because that means you'll never see that person again.

DONNA. You won't see that person forever? That's just too corny to believe.

TY. I believe it sort of—I always say "Later"—I never say "Goodbye."

(Time passes.)

THE CLINIC—June 23rd

DONNA. Eight years old, I think. So, Father O'Brian said that saying five "Hail Marys," five "Our Fathers," and five "Glory Bes," on All Saints' Day would get a soul out of Purgatory.

TY. All Souls' Day.

DONNA. Right. All Souls'. So, I got this great idea to get Marilyn Monroe out of Purgatory. So, I said a Rosary for her. And I had this thing for Clark Gable, so I said a Rosary for him. And Ernie Kovaks had just died ...

TY. Ernie Kovaks and Clark Cable?

DONNA. And Marilyn Monroe. They all made it to Heaven the same day.

(Time passes into night. TY sits on the tree stump, stage right, smoking a cigarette. DONNA, sneaking out after hours, enters from the stage right fence.)

THE CLINIC—June 24th, 2:30 a.m.

DONNA. Can I bum a cigarette?

TY. This is your fault.

DONNA. No. You choose to smoke.

TY. I haven't smoked in eight years and now I meet you and puff, puff. I'm the fucking little engine that could. Artie would say you're a bad influence.

DONNA. Artie wouldn't know a bad influence if he saw it in the mirror.

TY. If it wasn't for Artie I wouldn't be here.

DONNA. Thanks a lot, Artie. *(Crosses to the card castle.)*

TY. I mean I wouldn't be alive to be here.

DONNA. Can I have one?

TY. Sure.

(TY tosses DONNA a pack of Merits.)

DONNA. Sissy cigarettes.

(DONNA takes a cigarette and tosses the package back to TY.)

TY. I beg your pardon?

DONNA. What are these? Merits? Give me another one. I'll do two at once.

TY. Why don't you just tear off the filter, butch?

DONNA. High school boys smoke Merits.

TY. I'm not a high school boy.

DONNA. Sweet Holy Mary, I already did that once.

TY. Did what?

DONNA. Nothing.

TY. What did you do once?

DONNA. What are you talking about?

TY. You said, "I already did that once." What?

DONNA. Has Roger had a listen yet?

TY. Okay. Okay.

DONNA. Has he?

TY. The Sex Sonar was by about twenty minutes ago.

DONNA. I'm good at this sneaking around. I should have been a bad kid.

TY. Roger warned me about having a relationship with you.

DONNA. He pulled me aside too. What did he say to you?

TY. He was real formal.

DONNA. Not with me. He said if we didn't cool it, I'd find my tush on the road to Indiana before I was ready.

TY. He told me that fraternizing with the opposite sex could lead to unhealthy romantic involvement.

DONNA. Son of a bitch thinks I'm trying to seduce you.

TY. I don't want us to get kicked out.

DONNA. We're not going to let anything happen.
You are really cute when you get all nervous.

TY. Cute? Cute? I haven't been cute in years.

DONNA. Maybe it's the moonlight.

TY. Cute? Are you trying to seduce me?

DONNA. "You can't chase a rabbit if it ain't runnin'."

TY. Nights are beautiful up here.

DONNA. Quiet.

TY. There aren't any crickets.

DONNA. There aren't, are there?

TY. You know what else I haven't seen? Maple trees. Just Aspen trees.

DONNA. There's a woman down on the street by the Imperial, she has maples planted and a gazebo and stained glass windows on her house.

TY. Dooley was talking about her—she's like got her own religion or something.

DONNA. Dooley would know.

TY. Maybe we should pay this woman a visit.

DONNA. No. No way. Right now I'd believe in anything if I thought I'd feel better.

TY. Body, then mind, then spirit?

DONNA. Okay, A.A. makes some sense.

TY. What do you mean, feel better?

DONNA. I have a lot to "make amends" for, you know, step number nine.

TY. Hook, line, and sinker—Roger's got to you.

DONNA. How do I give Devan back six years?

TY. Show up to court sober.

DONNA. In Estelle's coin ceremony—you said that, when we passed the coin around, you said you liked the way she was always so up, so happy.

TY. I'll miss her. Good old perky Estelle.

DONNA. What will you say about me at my coin ceremony—when I leave? "I like Donna because she's always in a foul mood."

TY. I like Donna because she's always in a foul mood, she taught me to smoke, she doesn't talk to anyone but me, and she kissed on our first date.

DONNA. I sound like a very generous girl.

TY. Generous girls are my favorite.

DONNA. Generous rich boys are my favorite.

(DONNA crosses to center. TY follows.)

TY. Kelly said you were watching me do the dishes today.

DONNA. I wasn't.

TY. I like it when you watch me.

DONNA. I don't watch you.

TY. I'm only four years younger than you.

DONNA. Age and weight are subjects we should avoid.

TY. If that thing, that thing you did before has anything to do with falling in love ...

DONNA. Whoa! Whoa! Whoa! Where. When. How did love ... Age, weight and love—off limits, okay?

TY. Listen, it's not just lust. I'm well acquainted with lust. Lust could not sustain me this long. Lust was Estelle.

DONNA. You lusted after Estelle? Perky, bouncy Estelle?

TY. She was nice.

DONNA. Don't talk to me. I'm not in the same camp as cute, perky, bouncy, nice Estelle. Don't talk.

TY. No, you're right. You're different than Estelle. The thing is ...

DONNA. The thing is, Ty, a woman can't be too flattered that you're interested in her. Because, frankly, Ty, based on what you've said in group, you seem to be interested in anything that has evolved beyond the salamander.

TY. I'm not talking interest here. I'm talking love. Love that only happens once or maybe twice if you're lucky.

DONNA. Like all good things, Ty, love is not inevitable but has to be chosen to make good sense.

TY. I choose you, then. And that's rare.

DONNA. Maybe it's not love.

TY. If it walks like a duck, looks like a duck, and quacks like a duck. It's a duck.

DONNA. You love me like a duck?

TY. I love you.

DONNA. It's not what you're saying, it's how ...

TY. How do you want me to say it?

DONNA. Like you don't say it to somebody every night.

TY. See, love is like a cricket in the mountains.

DONNA. (*Trying not to laugh.*) Love is like a cricket in the mountains?

TY. See, love is like a cricket in the mountains.

DONNA. (*Laughing at Ty.*) There are no crickets in the mountains.

TY. I meant as rare as ... We might never have a chance to fall in love again—this might be our last chance. We're not teenagers anymore.

DONNA. Age and love in one breath. Now, say "fat" and I'll clock you.

Ty? Ty, don't pout. I'm just teasing you.

TY. What are you so afraid of?

DONNA. Spiders.

Big time wrestlers.

Public speaking.

TY. Me.

DONNA. You.

TY. Us.

DONNA. Some people don't make it, Ty. We aren't supposed to feel like this ... Mark did and he's dead, Ty. Dead. All he did was fall in love too soon, too fast ... Roger's got lists of people who compromised their sobriety by falling in love and they died, Ty. They died; sad, lonely, drunks.

TY. I won't let anything happen to you. They sell you that *Romeo And Juliet* stuff, 'cause some people really need it. But we, us, come on ... We're not stupid. It wasn't love at first sight or anything ...

DONNA. No, it wasn't that.

TY. Want to go steady?

DONNA. Let's look for a shooting star.

(TY takes Donna's hand. THEY hold hands and look at the sky. Time changes to the present. Suddenly TY leaves the clinic for the studio. HE staples a new canvas to his studio wall as HE speaks.)

THE STUDIO

TY. This is it! This is what I can paint. I am the thing that's missing in your portrait! I can picture us, together.

DONNA. It's not what happened, Ty.

TY. No! You can't talk back to me now. You didn't talk when I needed you. It's too late for you now. This is my memory. You are in my memory. You can't just change the rules. This is what *I* remember.

DONNA. It wasn't the start of anything. We didn't see a shooting star.

TY. Shooting stars are for Hallmark cards.

DONNA. Other things happened.

TY. What the hell does that mean?

DONNA. You know, Ty. (*Goes into the house.*)

TY. (*To the audience.*) Fifty percent of rehab patients ultimately die of drink or drugs. At least once a week Roger would recite the fifty percent statistics and warn that the possibility of returning to active addiction increased with blah, blah, blah; blah, blah, blah and establishing a romantic relationship within one year of sobriety.

(DONNA enters and starts working frantically on her card castle. TY watches her from the steps.)

THE CLINIC—June 26, 1:00 p.m.

DONNA. Roger is about as sensitive as a blacksmith's shoe.

TY. How did you want him to say it?

DONNA. He didn't have to say, "She was dumb. She knew her boyfriend was an addict. You be that stupid, you'll O. D. too."

TY. At least he didn't call her "perky and bouncy."

DONNA. She wasn't dead when I called her that. (*Crosses stage left.*) Sorry I didn't see you last night.

TY. Were you mad about something?

DONNA. No. I actually slept through the night. My first time.

TY. I know, I slipped upstairs and peeked in at you.

DONNA. Ty, you could be suspended for that.

TY. I missed you.

DONNA. It's probably better not to do that anymore.

TY. Sneak out? Not meet anymore?

DONNA. I think it's better ...

TY. I really like it.

DONNA. It's sort of adolescent.

TY. Ya, it is. You're right. (*Crosses to Donna.*) We could sit together at meals, you know.

DONNA. People will talk.

TY. So?

DONNA. I'm not a hussy.

TY. Who said you're a hussy?

DONNA. If the captain of the baseball team got you pregnant, you'd be sensitive too.

TY. If the captain of the baseball team got me pregnant, I'd be very sensitive.

DONNA. Besides, why sit with me? You seem to like to flirt with Viki over chicken pot pie.

TY. Her father owns one of the best clubs in New York.

DONNA. So, she's someone who thinks you're famous? (*CHIMES ring.*) I'll sit with you tomorrow, at breakfast.

(DONNA kisses Ty on the forehead and exits. TY addresses the audience from his studio.)

THE STUDIO

TY. Donna was the subject in group.

(DONNA is seen, sitting in a chair, through the window of the house.)

THE CLINIC, June 28, 10:30 a.m.

DONNA. *(In group.)* And I'd call in to work for him, if he had a hang over. Say he was sick.

TY. "Group" is not a support meeting like A.A. "Group" is confrontational therapy.

DONNA. When he hit me, I lied about the bruises. When he didn't come home, I blamed myself—even a good man prefers a beautiful woman. I certainly prefer a beautiful man. I've been hearing what you say to me, and you're right. I am as addicted to Brad as I am to drink. I would do anything for him—anything—and I thought that was love.

TY. Then Roger said, "Tell the group about Devan."

THE CLINIC, June 28, 10:30 a.m.

DONNA. Umm, I don't know what to say ... He made up this joke, "What do you call a dinosaur in the mud?"

TY. *(From his studio, as Roger.)* Why did you lose custody of him?

DONNA. "Icky." Get it? A dinosaur in the mud? "Icky?" He made it up by himself.

There's a law in Indiana. Alcoholics automatically lose custody ...

TY. (*As Roger.*) You're avoiding my question.

DONNA. Roger, It's none of your damn business.

TY. (*As Roger.*) You're as sick as your secrets, lady.

DONNA. You're as stupid as your cliches, man.

TY. (*As Roger.*) Cut the bull shit!

DONNA. I locked him out of the house!

After supper, he'd go into the back yard and play. That's when I would drink, while I cleaned up the dishes. When I got into Valium. I passed out a few times because of the combination—pills and liquor—and he got locked out.

The last time it was cold, it was winter, and he slept on the door step—he almost froze to death. A neighbor found him.

He didn't go for help because he didn't want to "Tell on his Mommy."

He's only six years old, but he's an expert at secrets.

THE STUDIO

TY. We didn't have our secret meetings anymore ...

(*Time passes. TY is lost in thought. Donna's line brings him back to the moment. THEY play "war" sitting on the ground in front of their chairs. The winner scoops up the cards and places them in a pile. DONNA plays the first card.*)

THE CLINIC—July 1st, 4:30 p.m.

DONNA. Go ahead.

TY. Ace.

DONNA. Eight.

TY. I win.

DONNA. Two.

TY. King. I win.

DONNA. Six.

TY. Ten. I win.

DONNA. Do you have to say "I win" every time? Ten.

TY. Only when, Jack, I win!

DONNA. Three.

TY. Five. I love this game.

DONNA. Seven.

TY. Ace. I win.

DONNA. Please stop saying that.

TY. Okay. Okay.

DONNA. Queen.

TY. King.

DONNA. If you're going to look like that, you might as well just say it.

TY. Okay. I win!

DONNA. Two.

TY. Two? I win without even putting down a card.

DONNA. Put it down.

TY. You know I won.

DONNA. Ty, come on. I played a two of hearts.

TY. Okay.

Two of clubs.

DONNA. War! One, two, three, King.

TY. Two.

DONNA. I win all those cards.

TY. Jack.
DONNA. King.
TY. Jack.
DONNA. Six.

(THEY continue playing as THEY talk.)

TY. Do you think you'll ever get married again?
DONNA. I could, but why make a man that happy?
TY. What did Roger say about the trial?
DONNA. "No." He said it would be "Against Medical Advice to go to court." Considering my history. Roger says that to be there on July Fifth, I'd have to leave on the Fourth. He says holidays are more difficult ... Like anyone ever celebrates the Fourth of July.
TY. It seems very natural for a kid to celebrate "Independence" day without his mom—it seems right. So leave at night.
DONNA. I think Roger's right.
TY. We could bust out of here. You and me. We'll tunnel out of here and go see the little guy. We'll slip out just as it gets dusk and we'll take a private jet and we'll fly over fireworks all tne way. I bet we can find a really cool Bed and Breakfast right on the Ohio River.
DONNA. We don't have to sneak. We can leave anytime we want, I mean legally.
TY. You take all the romance out of everything.
DONNA. If we go, just like for twenty-four hours and you keep me sober and I keep you sober, well, maybe I could do it—get my boy Devan back.
TY. Roger won't like us going together.
DONNA. You're right. We can't go.

TY. You can go.

DONNA. I can't do it alone.

TY. Fuck it! I'll go with you and we'll get your kid.

DONNA. Devan'll like you.

TY. Good.

DONNA. He really needs a good man around him.

TY. I'm coming back here after we get him.

DONNA. But maybe you could visit when you're done. Devan really needs a friend like you. You could take him to baseball games and teach him to fish and all that stuff.

TY. Are you asking me to move to Indiana?

DONNA. No.

TY. How am I supposed to be this kid's father from New York?

DONNA. Devan has a father. He needs a friend.

TY. I mean, I don't think I'd be good with kids, Donna.

DONNA. I just thought you wanted to help Devan.

TY. I do. I want to help Devan.

(DONNA takes the cards.)

TY. Wait, you took that one and it was mine. That ten is mine, the nine was yours. I won that one.

DONNA. No, I put down the ten, I'm sure. I did.

TY. You weren't paying attention. You were talking.

DONNA. Oh, okay, whatever.

TY. No, I don't want it if you think I'm wrong.

DONNA. Take them.

TY. I'm not cheating. You're just like Artie. "Take them."

DONNA. We'll play war on them. Who ever wins the war gets them plus the extra cards.

TOGETHER. One, Two, Three ...

TY. Six.

DONNA. Three.

TY. I win!

DONNA. What's this? Somebody drew on this card.

TY. Oops!

DONNA. What is it? Broccoli?

TY. It's a tree. There's an ace with you on it.

DONNA. Oh?

TY. Naked.

DONNA. Let me see.

TY. I sold it to Dooley for a nickel.

DONNA. Only a nickel?

TY. The diamond was discreetly placed.

DONNA. Sex jokes don't become a man who's losing his hair.

TY. I'm losing my hair?

DONNA. Not much really.

TY. It's noticeable?

DONNA. It's gonna rain.

TY. Your card castle's going to get blown all over the place.

DONNA. No. I've been glueing the base together with nail polish.

TY. That's cheating.

DONNA. Who says?

TY. Well it seems like ...

DONNA. It seems like ... what ever works. *(DONNA unconsciously ruffles the edge of the cards several times.)*

TY. I hate the rain.

DONNA. I like it—makes everything smell new.

TY. It makes the world feel small. (*Referring to the ruffling of the cards.*) Could you not do that?

DONNA. If we go see Devan together—you've got to know something ...

TY. Okay ...?

DONNA. Ty, Ty, it can't be a romantic trip. It can't.

TY. Why?

(The CHIMES ring.)

DONNA. It's not like I don't want it to be ... It's just that ...

TY. You kissed on the first date.

DONNA. The judge will know ... (*DONNA exits.*)

THE STUDIO

TY. I can't say she lead me on. That's when I started to talk to my roommate Dooley about Donna. Dooley had snorted, smoked, and drank his way around the comedy club circuit and drifted into minor celebrity. Dooley said Donna sounded "bye-sexual." "When you get sexual, she says 'Bye.'"

(TY enters the scene as DONNA enters from the front door. SHE is agitated.)

THE CLINIC, July 3rd, 6:30 p.m.

DONNA. That was really, really stupid, Ty.

TY. (*Still to the audience.*) Dooley was dead within a year after we left Colorado.

DONNA. Really stupid.

TY. "Live fast, die young, and make a good looking corpse."

DONNA. How can you be so dumb?

THE CLINIC. July 3rd, 6:30 p.m.

TY. What?

DONNA. Roger saw that.

TY. I just winked.

DONNA. That was not just a wink, that was a, a come hither look.

TY. A come hither look? I did that? I gave you a come hither look?

DONNA. A very adult come hither look.

TY. Harsh.

DONNA. Roger just said we're spending too much time together.

TY. So, what's the problem? Now you decide to listen to him?

DONNA. It's not that.

TY. You've been, been, been avoiding me, again.

DONNA. Oh, that's not true. That's not like me at all, no ...

TY. You, you, you don't lie about the inside things, remember-remember-remember?

DONNA. (*Realizes that Ty is drunk.*) Ty?

TY. Oh, come on.

DONNA. How? Where did it come from?

TY. You're nagging.

DONNA. Was it "Teachers"? "Wild Turkey"?

TY. The strongest thing I've had is turkey pot pie. Scout's honor.

DONNA. Kiss me.

TY. No. Someone might see.

DONNA. You're afraid I'll taste it.

TY. I'm, I'm, I'm afraid you'll bite me.

DONNA. Look me in the eye and say that you are sober.

TY. Donna, you are sober.

DONNA. You saved some bottles from the plane.

TY. This is the first time.

DONNA. Goodbye Devan.

TY. Donna, don't.

DONNA. Now, I can't even see my little boy.

TY Of course you can. Don't get all dramatic.

DONNA. I can't trust you. You promised I could ...

TY. This is no big deal. Dooley's been giving me a lot of shit. And, and and Roger's really got a bug up his ass about ...

DONNA. I wanted to count on you!

TY. Me or just somebody!?!

(CHIMES.)

DONNA. Did you love your girlfriend?

TY. The chimes just rang. We've got an A. A. meeting.

DONNA. Did you love Julie?

TY. What? You, you, you going to tell Roger I'm drunk if I don't answer your questions?

DONNA. Did you do this to her?

TY. We'll talk later, I just wanted to ask about Devan's trial.

DONNA. Listen to me. Did you ever love her?

TY. I think so, at first, in the beginning.

DONNA. The only person you've ever said you loved was Artie.

TY. Oh, Artie.

DONNA. Yes, Artie.

TY. You're not jealous of Artie, for God's sake.

DONNA. Did you love him?

TY. I slept with him, Donna.

DONNA. I know you slept with him.

TY. He didn't infect me if that's what you're worried about.

DONNA. Listen to me.

TY. Three hundred negative tests ...

DONNA. Did you love him?

TY. I didn't love Julie.

DONNA. Artie.

TY. I think I loved Artie, sure.

DONNA. You don't remember?

TY. I was a kid. Artie gave me food, clothing, shelter, art, self respect. Artie loved me. I could love Artie—it was something, the only thing, I could do for him.

DONNA. You make him sound like a charity case.

TY. I don't know. I don't know what you want me to say to that.

We're going to be late.

DONNA. I want you to say what you love.

TY. There are things that I love and there are things that I hate—sometimes they are the same things.

DONNA. Did you love him most?

TY. Did you love Brad most? Did you ever wonder what would have happened if you thought you were worthwhile enough to love an adult?

DONNA. Do you think you're worthwhile enough to love a person?

TY. If you have a problem with my sexual preference...

DONNA. Ty, your sexual preference isn't the problem. The problem is you have no preference.

It's not whether you have had sex with a man or a woman. It's that so far you don't prefer, you don't love anyone more than a bottle of booze.

You seduce and flirt and con—but it's all about getting numb.

(TY collapses in frustration. HE kneels center.)

TY. Donna, I don't know what the con is anymore.

DONNA. What's the truth then?

TY. I don't want to live without you.

DONNA. Ty, it looks like love, it feels like love, it acts like love ...

TY. It is love.

DONNA. It's addiction.

TY. I thought you were going to say "it's a duck."

DONNA. You've got no guts, Ty. You try to fill that hole with booze, drugs, paint, lonely people.

TY. How am I supposed to fill it?

DONNA. Brad used to say that I was his "better half." That was our problem. We were two half people trying to be one person.

TY. I can't live without you, Donna. *(Stands.)*

DONNA. You're still half a person, Ty.

TY. You're just talking the program. I'm talking us. You're just leaning on the program like some damn ...

DONNA. It's all I have left to lean on. And it's right, Ty. It's God damn right!

TY. Someday, I'll pick up again if you're not there. Someday, I'll eat all those colors and it will work—it will kill me because you aren't there.

DONNA. That's your choice. You can kill yourself, but not me. (*Starts to exit into the house.*)

TY. You should go alone to see Devan, you can.

DONNA. I don't have the money.

TY. I'll give you the money.

DONNA. I don't know how to get there.

TY. I'll arrange it.

DONNA. I don't want anything from you.

TY. Why won't you go?

DONNA. I don't want to hurt him like you just hurt me.

Devan's the only thing keeping me alive.

TY. You don't want a son, you want a life support system. You just said ...

DONNA. Tomorrow's too soon.

TY. You've done more than full term here. You're just hiding out.

I'll have a car come up to meet you.

DONNA. No.

TY. Damn it, Donna. Let me do something for you. For just once in my life, let me do something for someone else.

DONNA. First get sober, Ty.

TY. We can always send the car away if you want.

You never asked Roger, did you?

DONNA. No.

TY. Pack your bag, meet me here during the dance, like ten—after it gets going. (*DONNA starts to leave.*) Donna, I still love you.

DONNA. I choose my son before you and before alcohol.

TY. What if our love is rare as a shooting star?

DONNA. Shooting stars happen all the time.

TY. I never see them.

(*DONNA exits. TY calls after her.*)

TY. Donna, don't tell Roger about the booze!

THE STUDIO

(*During the following, TY puts on a sports jacket and gets a present for Donna. It is night. Classic rock and roll plays inside the house—it is the same SONG that we heard on Ty's boom box at the top of the play.*)

TY. She told Roger. No more little secrets. Roger called Donna giving me bloody hell my first real intervention. You see, you have to learn that you hurt the people that love you when you drink. Finally, someone loved me enough to tell me that I was killing myself, but I wasn't going to kill her. Artie never told me. Artie made them heros; Van Gogh, Hemingway, Artaud, Byron, Cocteau, James Dean, Jackson Pollock, Mark Rothko, Tennesee Williams, the list is endless ... The great, dead, drugged and drunken, heroes. Better to die in a blaze of glory like them; like Artie, than to fade away. See, that's the terrible hoax. That's the big secret because every single one of them died sad and sick. They died cheated of their prime. They died engulfed in the nightmare they thought would inspire them. They died, every one of them, with the same last airy words—I want to live I want to live I want to live I want to live I want to live.

Roger gave me a choice of suspension from the clinic or starting the program from the beginning. On July Fourth, three years ago, I re-started the program.

(DONNA enters from the porch door in a dress. SHE stands on the porch with her suitcase watching for TY.)

TY. I took the money I had in my shoe, made arrangements for Donna. And turned the rest of my secret cash over to Roger.

THE CLINIC—July 4th, 10:15 p.m.

DONNA. You couldn't get it?

TY. It'll be right here.

DONNA. You said ten and it's after and I thought it wasn't coming.

TY. I got it.

DONNA. They say never to believe someone when they've been drinking.

TY. You look great.

DONNA. Really?

TY. You can believe it, I'm sober, tonight.

DONNA. I don't want Devan to be embarrassed.

TY. I'm sorry I picked up the other night.

DONNA. We always are.

TY. I need more than that.
DONNA. No. It's too hard.
TY. I totally forgot they were there.
DONNA. Bull shit!
TY. Sorry. Sorry. That was the addict talking. Sorry.
DONNA. What if I'm not ready?
TY. Roger thinks you are.
DONNA. And you?
TY. You are.
DONNA. But what if ...
TY. That's that "what if" we have to live with, isn't it?
DONNA. When'd you get so smart?

(FIREWORKS bathe the stage in colors.)

DONNA. Look!
TY. I got something for you.

(TY hands her the box. DONNA opens the box.)

DONNA. Ty, it's just what I've always pictured.
(DONNA puts on the corsage.)
TY. Are you in love with me now? You promised.
DONNA. No. But I'd go to the prom with you.

*(THEY slow dance. THEY kiss. DONNA gently pushes
    Ty away.)*

TY. So, this is how people do it? They meet and talk
and fight and talk and then they go to the prom.

DONNA. I think it would be nice if Devan took after you. I'd like my boy to be like you, Ty. Except when he's playing cards.

TY. (*Crosses to the castle.*) You've got to put the ace of spades on top of your ... hut—before you go.

DONNA. No. I'm only done with the foundation.

TY. I'll finish it for you.

DONNA. Build your own.

TY. Donna does not play well with others.

DONNA. Here you can have my ace of spades.

TY. Someday, I can visit you, I can put it on top of your new castle. I'll hold onto it until then. I'll hold on and never let it go.

DONNA. (*Frightened, sees the car.*) Oh, Ty, a limousine! (*Crosses back to her suitcase on the porch.*) Goodbye, Ty.

TY. No, just say, "later."

(*TY still holding the card addresses the audience. HE crosses to the studio.*)

THE STUDIO

TY. She knew it was forever.

DONNA. (*Still on the porch.*) Goodbye, Ty.

TY. Do you still think about me?

DONNA. Sometimes. Do you still love me?

TY. I did love you, Donna.

For the first time, I know, I really did love a person, I really can love a person.

DONNA. Now you know, Ty.

TY. (*Rips the ace of spades in half and lets it fall to the floor.*) Goodbye. Goodbye, Donna.

(*DONNA poses as the stage becomes her portrait. TY sees the portrait. HE admires it for a moment. Exhausted and elated, TY addresses the audience.*)

TY. A painting, a picture, a portrait. A portrait of a woman on a bone white Victorian porch, wearing love on her wrist and new beginnings bursting all out, all over the sky.

END OF PLAY

COSTUME PLOT

DONNA	TY
Beige Slacks	Ripped Blue Jeans
Oversized Print Shirt, Earth Tones	Blue Pull-over Shirt w/ Collar
Cream Cardigan Sweater	Ripped Denim Shirt w/ Pocket, Worn Open
Keds Tennis Shoes	
Simple Dress, Floral Print (quick change)	Converse High Tops, Blue
Comfortable Dress Shoes (quick change)	Sports Jacket

PROPERTY LIST

DONNA	TY
Card Castle, rigged to collapse (table on stage)	Boom Box (paint table)
Extra Cards (table on stage)	Brushes, 1 practical (paint table)
Twinkie, partially eaten, edible (w/ Donna)	Pizza Box Palette, (studio floor)
Clip Board w/ paper & pen (on wall of house)	Canvas w/ Beginnings of Painting, (studio wall)
Afghan (chair SR)	Staple Gun, practical (paint table)
Cigarettes, Camels w/o filter, (Sweater Pocket)	Oil Paint, practical (paint table)
Lighter, practical, (Sweater Pocket)	Oil Paint, edible frosting, (paint table)
Small Area Rug (off SR)	Ace of Spades (denim shirt pocket)
Large Flower Pot (SR Steps)	Ace of Spades (card castle table)
Hand Spade (in pot)	
Bag of Dirt (in pot)	Package of Certs, edible (pants pocket)
Beans in a Bowl, edible (Porch SR)	Cigarettes, Merits, practical (off SR)
Paint Scraper, (Porch SR)	
Four Trash Bags, stuffed (off SR)	Lighter, practical (off SR)
Laundry Basket w/7 unfolded sheets, (off SR)	House Paint Can (Porch SR)
Coffee Mug (off SR)	House Paint Brush, in can (SR Porch)
Deck of Cards, in war order (off SR)	
Suitcase (off SR)	

TY contd.

Potatoes In Bowl, one to peel (SR Porch)

Potato Peeler, in bowl (SR Porch)

Place Mat & Pencil (on paint table)

Picnic Blanket (off SR)

Deck of Cards, in war order (Denim shirt pocket)

Box w/ Corsage, practical (under paint table)

SET NOTE

Because this is a memory play, the set may be selectively realistic, reflecting the painter's imagination rather than strict reality. It is imperative that the set allow a free flow of time and action.

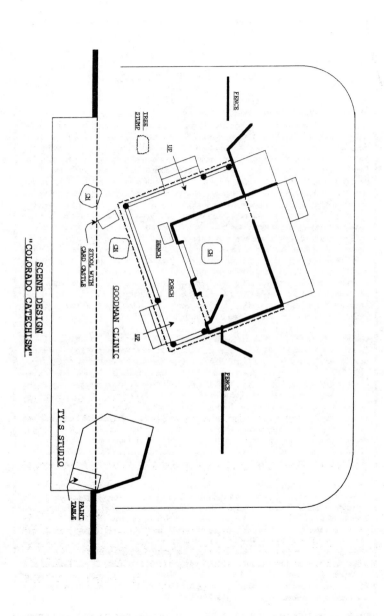

SCENE DESIGN
"COLORADO CATECHISM"

NEW COMEDIES FROM
SAMUEL FRENCH, INC.

MAIDS OF HONOR. (Little Theatre.) Comedy. Joan Casademont. 3m., 4f. Comb Int./Ext. Elizabeth McGovern, Laila Robins and Kyra Sedgwick starred in this warm, wacky comedy at Off-Broadway's famed WPA Theatre. Monica Bowlin, a local TV talk-show host, is getting married. Her two sisters, Isabelle and Annie, are intent on talking her out of it. It seems that Mr. Wonderful, the groom-to-be, is about to be indicted for insider trading, a little secret he has failed to share with his fiancee, Monica. She has a secret she has kept herself, too—she's pregnant, possibly not by her groom-to-be! All this is uncovered by delightfully kookie Isabelle, who aspires to be an investigative reporter. She'd also like to get Monica to realize that she is marrying the wrong man, for the wrong reason. She should be marrying ex-boyfriend Roger Dowling, who has come back to return a diary Monica left behind. And sister Annie should be marrying the caterer for the wedding, old flame Harry Hobson—but for some reason she can't relax enough to see how perfect he is for her. The reason for all three Bowlin women's difficulties with men, the reason why they have always made the wrong choice and failed to see the right one, is that they are the adult children of an alcoholic father and an abused mother, both now passed away, and they cannot allow themselves to love because they themselves feel unlovable. Sound gloomy and depressing? No, indeed. This delightful, wise and warm-hearted new play is loaded with laughs. We would also like to point out to all you actors that the play is also loaded with excellent monologues, at least one of which was recently included in an anthology of monologues from the best new plays.) **(#14961)**

GROTESQUE LOVESONGS. (Little Theatre.) Comedy. Don Nigro. (Author of *The Curate Shakespeare As You Like It, Seascape with Sharks and Dancer* and other plays). This quirky new comedy about a family in Terre Haute, Indiana, enchanted audiences at NYC's famed WPA Theatre. Two brothers, Pete and John, live with their parents in a big old house with an attached greenhouse. The father, Dan, has a horticulture business. A pretty young woman named Romy is more or less engaged to marry younger brother Johnny as the play begins, and their prospects look quite rosy, for Johnny has just inherited a ton of money from recently-deceased family friend, Mr. Agajanian. Why, wonders Pete, has Agajanian left his entire estate to Johnny? He starts to persistently ask this question to his mother, Louise. Eventually, Louise does admit that, in fact, Mr. Agajanian was Johnny's father. This news stuns Johnny; but he's not *really* staggered until he goes down to the greenhouse and finds Pete and Romy making love. Pete, it seems, has always desperately wanted Romy; but when she chose Johnny instead he married a woman in the circus who turned out to be a con artist, taking him for everything he had and then disappearing. It seems everyone but Johnny is haunted by a traumatic past experience: Louise by her affair with Agajanian; Dan by the memory of his first true love, a Terre Haute whore; Pete by his failed marriage, and Romy by her *two* failed marriages. (One husband she left; the other was run over by a truckload of chickens [He loved cartoons so much, says Romy, that it was only fitting he should die like Wile E. Coyote.]). And, each character but Johnny knows what he wants. Louise and Dan want the contentment of their marriage; Romy wants to bake bread in a big old house—and she wants Pete, who finally admits that he wants her, too. And, finally, Johnny realizes what he wants. He does not want the money, or Agajanian's house. He wants to go to Nashville to make his own way as a singer of sad—yes, grotesque—love songs in the night. NOTE: this play is a treasure-trove of scene and monologue material.) **(#9925)**